Just the Facts
Racism

Adrian Cooper

www.heinemann.co.uk/library
Visit our website to find out more information about **Heinemann Library** books.

To order:
 Phone 44 (0) 1865 888066
 Send a fax to 44 (0) 1865 314091
 Visit the Heinemann Bookshop at www.heinemann.co.uk/library to browse our catalogue and order online.

Produced by Monkey Puzzle Media Ltd
Gissing's Farm, Fressingfield, Suffolk IP21 5SH, UK

First published in Great Britain by Heinemann Library, Halley Court, Jordan Hill, Oxford OX2 8EJ, part of Harcourt Education.
Heinemann is a registered trademark of Harcourt Education Ltd.

First published in paperback in 2004
© Harcourt Education Ltd 2003
The moral right of the proprietor has been asserted.

Editorial: Patience Coster
Design: Jamie Asher
Picture Research: Lynda Lines
Illustration: Michael Posen
Production: Viv Hichens

Originated by Dot Gradations Ltd
Printed and bound in China by South China Printing Company

ISBN 0 431 16140 2 (hardback)
07 06 05 04 03
10 9 8 7 6 5 4 3 2

ISBN 0 431 16148 8 (paperback)
08 07 06 05 04 03
10 9 8 7 6 5 4 3 2 1

British Library Cataloguing in Publication Data
Cooper, Adrian
Racism
305.8
A full catalogue record for this book is available from the British Library.

Acknowledgements
The publishers would like to thank the following for permission to reproduce photographs:
AKG London pp. **1**, **10**, **12**, **14**, **17**; Ancient Art and Architecture Collection p. **7**; Associated Press pp. **36**, (Dita Alangkara), **36** (Santiago Lyon); Camera Pres p. **22**; Corbis p. **27** (Steve Chenn); Corbis Stock Market p. **9** (Ronnie Kaufman); David Hoffmann Photo Library pp. **5 bottom** (Nick Cobbing), **5 top**, **37**; John Birdsall Photography p. **50**; Popperfoto pp. **16**, **28 bottom** (Reuters), **43 bottom** (Mike Hutchings/Reuters); Rex Features pp. **19 bottom** (Robert W Kelly/Timepix), **21** (Mirek Towski), **24**, **25**, **30** (Nils Jorgensen), **31** (Terry Thompson), **34** (MXL), **43 top** (Marcus Zeffler), **44–45** (Richard Young); Topham Picturepoint pp. **6–7** (Image Works), **7**, **15**, **19 top**, **28 top** (Prosport), **32** (Image Works), **38** (Image Works), **39** (Image Works), **41** (PA/John Stillwell), **47** (Image Works), **48–49** (Image Works).

Cover photograph reproduced with permission of Format/Ulrike Press.

Every effort has been made to contact copyright holders of any material reproduced in this book. Any omissions will be rectified in subsequent printings if notice is given to the publishers.

Any words appearing in the text in bold, **like this**, are explained in the Glossary.

Contents

What is racism?.................................... 4

Race and racists................................... 6

What is race?..................................... 8

Racism in history

The slave trade.................................10

Colonialism 12

The 'science' of race............................14

Government of race: Nazi Germany...........16

Resisting racism.................................18

Racism in society

Our multi-ethnic world 20

Racism and the legal system....................24

Racism at work.................................26

Racism and sport 28

The media and race............................30

The media and migration......................32

The arguments about racism

Citizens of the world?..........................34

Institutional racism 36

What is being done?

The global community against racism.......40

The end of apartheid...........................42

Who else is tackling racism?..................44

Racism and you

Ask yourself: Who am I?.......................46

Experiences of racism..........................48

Facts and figures...............................50

Further information.............................52

Glossary..54

Index 56

What is racism?

'Racist' people believe that personality and behaviour are linked to physical characteristics. Because they believe in this link, racists base their judgement of a person's abilities or intelligence on the shape of that person's face or on skin colour. Racists are also usually convinced that other **ethnic groups** or **nationalities** are inferior to their own. This false attitude of superiority is known as racism.

Racism can take the form of a casual joke between friends, using **stereotypes** as the basis for the joke; it can be graffiti on a street wall, or chants at a football match. At its most extreme, racism may mean that somebody is murdered because of the colour of his or her skin.

What is racial discrimination?

Racial **discrimination** is a kind of behaviour. It treats one person less favourably than another on grounds of race, colour, nationality or ethnic or racial origins. This is called direct discrimination.

Indirect racial discrimination happens where people are treated according to the same rules as each other, but the effect of the rules is to disadvantage a particular racial group. For example, to refuse a black person a job because of his or her black skin is direct discrimination. But if a job is restricted to people who attended a particular school, and that school has always had only white or nearly all white pupils, that is known as indirect discrimination.

What is ethnicity?

An ethnic group shares a cultural or national history, for example, **Roma** peoples, Spanish-Americans in the USA, Polish-descended citizens in the USA, Italian-descended citizens in Australia and **Kosovans** in the UK.

> **"All human beings are born free and equal, without distinction of any kind, such as race, colour, sex, language, religion, political or other opinion, national or social origin, property, birth or other status."**
>
> From the Universal Declaration of Human Rights, United Nations (1948).

What is institutional racism?

When the workings of an institution, like a business or a public body, encourage racially discriminatory results, even without the people working in that institution being racists, there is said to be institutional racism.

Racism can affect individuals and disrupt **communities** in many ways. It's not just individual people who are racist. History shows that some of the worst crimes against humanity have been committed by governments that have created societies based on racism. For much of the 20th century, the apartheid regime in South Africa treated black people as inferior to whites. In Nazi Germany between 1933 and 1945, and more recently in the countries that used to make up Yugoslavia, the political leaders and governments discriminated against and killed entire communities because they belonged to a certain 'race'. This ugly extreme of racism is called 'ethnic cleansing' or '**genocide**'.

Racist graffiti, spray-painted on to a wall in Poland.

When racism surfaces, like at this demonstration in the UK, it creates racial tension and often leads to violence.

5

Race and racists

Racism: a fact of history

Racism is one of the most important issues facing the world today. It affects the schools we go to, sports we follow, **communities** we call home and countries we live in. Some people are affected by racism every single day, and when this happens it stops them from achieving their individual potential, cuts their dreams short and makes their lives miserable.

By looking at the past we can often find similarities or connections that help our understanding of the world today. The history of racism reminds us that terrible acts of violence and suffering can grow from a fear or dislike of people who are 'different'. But it is also important to remember that reacting against racism has sparked positive changes in **civil** and **human rights**.

Learning from the past

We only need look around our own community – friends at school, people on television or next-door neighbours – to see how incredibly diverse people are. In fact, with more and more people from varying ethnic backgrounds living side by side, our societies are more diverse now than they've ever been. Our lives are enriched and inspired by athletes, writers, artists and musicians who have succeeded in multi-ethnic societies. But this doesn't mean that racism is a thing of the past: **discrimination**, racial crimes and violence are facts of the present, too. Since the 1940s, the **United Nations** has encouraged **democracies** throughout the world to pass laws making racial discrimination unlawful. Today free, democratic societies such as those of Australia, the USA and Europe have passed civil rights and racial discrimination acts that make any sort of racist behaviour unlawful, whether it happens at work, in school or on the streets.

This book will look at periods of history that show how ugly racism can be and will illustrate why it is so important to make sure that racism is unlawful. It will also explain how racism affects our societies today, and why it is still important for us to recognize and tackle this kind of discrimination.

Persecuted because of their 'race': prisoners of war in Auschwitz concentration camp during World War Two.

❝I hate racial discrimination most intensely and all its manifestations.... I have cherished the ideal of a democratic and free society in which all persons live together in harmony and with equal opportunities.**❞**

Nelson Mandela, president of South Africa from 1994–99. Mandela was elected to office in South Africa's first ever multi-racial elections.

What is race?

For some people, race starts with the family: who their parents are, or their grandparents or their great-great grandparents. The various members of a person's family tree provide that person with valuable information about his or her **genes** and **DNA**. The chemicals in a person's DNA carry information from one generation to the next – for example, from mother to son. And it's this inherited information – a sort of personal map – that helps to explain why children often look like their parents, or why brothers and sisters have the same colour eyes. It also means that a person's physical features – the shape of face and body, the colour of hair, skin or eyes – are inherited from his or her ancestors. The inheritance of physical features is known as heredity.

Beyond the family

The world's population is more than six billion today, but every person on the planet is unique, with his or her very own DNA map (although identical twins share a DNA map). Despite this incredible diversity, all humans belong to the same group, or **species**, called *Homo sapiens*. This common name means that *all* of us share biological and genetic similarities. When people think about 'race' in this way, they often say things like: 'We're all part of the human race', or 'We're all human beings'.

However, some people understand the word 'race' to mean belonging to a certain group defined by certain physical characteristics, for example, black people in America, or every white person in Sydney, Australia. This way of understanding race can sometimes link a person's appearance with their personality or their ability. For example, someone might say: 'All Indian kids are

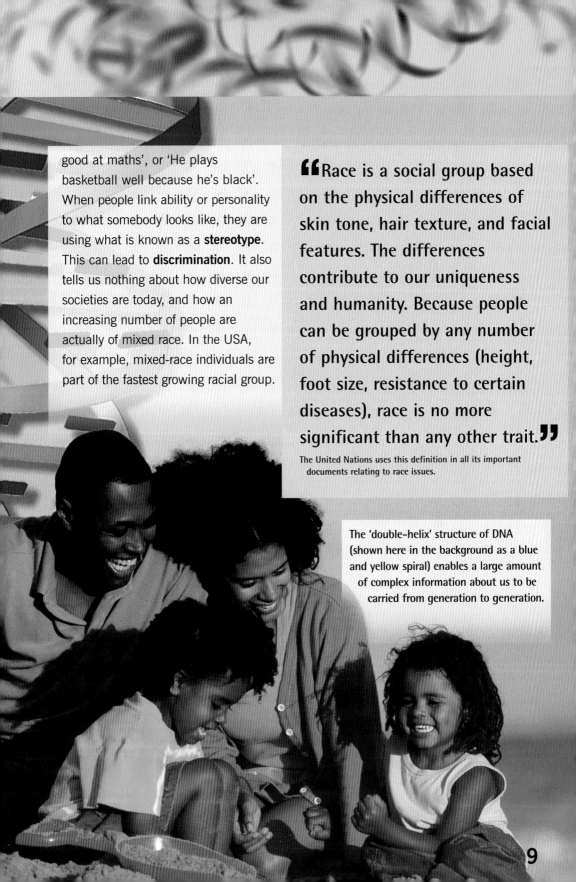

good at maths', or 'He plays basketball well because he's black'. When people link ability or personality to what somebody looks like, they are using what is known as a **stereotype**. This can lead to **discrimination**. It also tells us nothing about how diverse our societies are today, and how an increasing number of people are actually of mixed race. In the USA, for example, mixed-race individuals are part of the fastest growing racial group.

❝Race is a social group based on the physical differences of skin tone, hair texture, and facial features. The differences contribute to our uniqueness and humanity. Because people can be grouped by any number of physical differences (height, foot size, resistance to certain diseases), race is no more significant than any other trait.❞

The United Nations uses this definition in all its important documents relating to race issues.

The 'double-helix' structure of DNA (shown here in the background as a blue and yellow spiral) enables a large amount of complex information about us to be carried from generation to generation.

The slave trade

Slavery is the situation which arises when one person has absolute power over another. Slavery has existed for centuries. Throughout its long history, people have been forced to work in extremely harsh conditions for very low pay. Descriptions of slavery can be found in the Bible and the Qur'an, and it existed in the Greek empire (800–146 BCE) and the Roman empire (753 BCE–CE 455). West African kingdoms also kept slaves, and a thriving trade in East Africa was driven by sultans from the Middle East, who sold people across Persia (present-day Iran) and Mesopotamia (present-day Iraq). But although these examples of slavery led to people being treated terribly, historians do not consider them to be acts of racism. This is because the slave traders and masters were often from the same **ethnic** or racial **group** as the slaves. This was not, however, the case with the Atlantic Slave Trade.

Starting in the 16th century and involving several European countries, the Atlantic Slave Trade was the forced movement of people from Africa to the Americas. Although Arab and African traders were involved in capturing and selling slaves, the main driving force was Europe's demand for plantation workers in the Caribbean, Brazil and what is now North America. The European nations gained huge economic benefits from the slave trade.

Shackled on the shores of West Africa, men are paraded like goods in front of a European man at the height of the Atlantic Slave Trade in 1820.

Money made from slavery helped to finance the **Industrial Revolution** in Britain during the 18th century.

For the African people who were captured and sold into slavery, the experience was appalling. Each ship crossing the 'Middle Passage' (a name given to the Atlantic journey) carried between 250 and 600 people in very cramped conditions. Men were chained together, and women were transported in separate parts of the ships. At least one million people died from diseases like **dysentery** and **smallpox** during the Middle Passage. Those who survived were put to work on cotton, tobacco, sugar and rice plantations and were often treated cruelly by the European plantation owners. Historians estimate that, between the years 1450 and 1850, at least twelve million people were shipped across the Atlantic. Some historians even suggest that, in the same period, as many as 28 million people left Africa in 54,000 separate voyages.

'We ought to be considered as men'

Towards the end of the 18th century, 'slave uprisings' in the West Indies and a growing **abolitionist** movement in Europe marked the beginning of the end for slavery. The trade was abolished in Britain in 1807.

In 1861, the American Civil War began. According to Abraham Lincoln, who had just become the sixteenth president of the USA, this war was fought because: 'Government cannot endure permanently half slave, half free'. The conflict involved more than 190,000 black soldiers. When it ended in 1865, slavery was abolished via the 'Emancipation Declaration'. The Fourteenth (1868) and Fifteenth (1870) Amendments to the American Constitution meant that African Americans were officially recognized as US citizens and granted the right to vote.

"I looked around the ship.... With the loathsomeness of the stench and the crying together, I became so sick and low that I was not able to eat.... I now wished for the last friend, Death, to relieve me."

From The Interesting Narrative of the Life of Olaudah Equiano (1789). Books such as this, written by former slaves, helped to bring about an end to slavery. They drew people's attention to its cruel and inhumane practices.

Colonialism

At the end of the 19th century, many peoples in Africa, Asia, Australia and the West Indies were directly ruled by countries in Europe. They became known as 'colonies' or 'empires'. The powers that ruled these colonies included Britain, France, Spain, Germany, Holland, Belgium and Italy, with Britain controlling the largest empire. These powers believed that the colonies they governed were in need of European 'civilization', and were keen to develop economies, provide medicine and encourage education there. The colonial governments also wanted to increase their own wealth and power by exploiting the colonies. In particular, many political and business leaders believed that if Europe's economy was to continue to grow it needed extra resources, like cotton or steel, many of which could be obtained from the colonized lands.

Much of this colonial activity took place without the agreement of the local inhabitants. For example, when English ships first arrived in Australia in 1788, the Aboriginal people weren't consulted when the English settlers 'claimed' the land. Peoples in Africa experienced similar treatment. In 1884, at a conference in Berlin, the European colonial powers gathered to decide the national borders of the continent. Without the permission or involvement of the African peoples, the European leaders decided which portions of land should be allocated to the various European governments, and Africa was 'sliced up like a cake'.

German missionaries prepare to take over administration of the East Africa colony in 1891. Missionary stations such as these were scattered throughout the German empire.

Africa: the white man's burden

Throughout the 18th century, European leaders had encouraged early explorers in Africa to 'open the path for commerce and Christianity'. To raise money for these journeys, adventurers and missionaries often publicized their trips as the 'white man's burden'. By this they meant they believed that Africa was benighted by ignorance – a 'dark continent' – and that it was Europe's duty to free the 'native' people of 'heathen' religions. When the famous British explorer, David Livingstone, died in 1862, he requested that his tombstone should bear words to encourage others in Europe to follow his example, and rescue the 'natives' from the 'sore of the world'.

What the European explorers and leaders were blind to, however, were historical facts. Across Africa, Asia and Australia, advanced cultures already existed with their own distinct societies, art forms and religious beliefs. Instead of bringing 'civilization', the Europeans tended to bring culture-clash, even war. Battles were fought against the Zulus in southern Africa and Emperor Menelik of Abyssinia (already an ancient Christian kingdom). Instead of the word of the Bible, it was the power of the 'Maxim' machine-gun that enabled the Europeans to colonize parts of Africa.

Once colonial powers had settled, however, there were benefits. Some local people took European-style jobs – as police officers, soldiers or government clerks. There was an enormous amount of building: railways in East and southern Africa, roads, bridges and factories. Healthcare and education programmes helped to control diseases and encouraged children to read and write. But despite all this, racial **segregation** and **discrimination** were a part of colonial society. In Kenya, for example, Europeans kept the most powerful positions. And white **communities** lived separately from black communities, with white people enjoying the best conditions.

Native Americans

In 1883 the US government's Indian Religious Crimes Code virtually outlawed the religions and beliefs of some 240 different tribal groups across North America. As a result of the Code, the US government established Courts of Indian Offences to enforce 'civilized habits and pursuits'.

The 'science' of race

The origin and **evolution** of human beings has fascinated, baffled and intrigued people for centuries. In the 17th century, scientists such as Swedish-born Carolus Linnaeus (1707–1778) and French-born George Cuvier (1769–1832) designed elaborate ways of classifying the natural world, beginning with descriptions of the different physical features of plants and animals. By the 19th century, *Homo sapiens* was also classified, and divided into race categories like 'negroid', 'mongoloid' and 'caucasoid'. The science of race was born, and so were beliefs that help to explain the idea of European superiority during the Atlantic Slave Trade and colonialism.

An example from Carolus Linnaeus's Systema Naturae.

When Charles Darwin published *On the Origin of Species* in 1859, he declared that: 'Light will be thrown on the origin of man and his history'. But Darwin's description of evolution as 'the survival of the fittest' led some people to believe that the various human race categories were in a battle for evolution. This misreading of Darwin's writing encouraged and supported several European 'scientists' who believed that some human beings and races were more evolved than others. This way of thinking, which became known as **Social Darwinism**, tended to place white Europeans higher up the human evolutionary tree. Some even believed you could tell how 'evolved' or 'civilized' people were by measuring the size of their skulls!

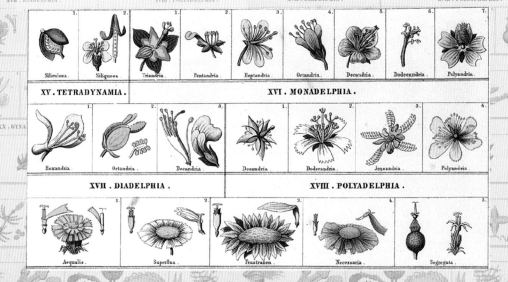

Race: the 'pseudo science'

After World War Two, a group of leading British scientists argued – by using modern **genetics** – that there wasn't any real science behind race theories. Because human beings had **migrated** across the Earth for thousands of years, it was impossible to classify people into 'races'. They suggested that the term **'ethnic group'** should be used instead of the word 'race'. Unlike 'race', which uses biological or physical characteristics to describe individual or group identity, the term 'ethnic group' emphasizes the national and cultural factors. The **United Nations** supported these discoveries, adding that there was 'no scientific evidence to prove humans differ in intelligence or emotional development based on race'. The ideas that may have seemed useful to people in the 18th and 19th centuries are now considered to be a **'pseudo'** science or 'scientific racism'.

Darwin's thinking

In his writings, Charles Darwin said that 'natural selection' was the driving power behind plant and animal evolution. He said that all organisms were in a constant struggle with others in the same species, and that those which survived through successive generations did so because of biological or physical traits that aided their survival. His ideas led some people to believe that the various human race categories were also in a battle for survival. They were adopted by several European 'scientists' who believed that some human beings and races were more evolved than others. But these theories about human evolution were a misunderstanding of Darwin's theory. Darwin's view of nature was not of a superior society, more perfect personality or civilized culture, but an entire **species** constantly adapting to changing environments in an endless process of evolution.

The observations and drawings that European explorers made during their travels influenced the science of race. Images of 'exotic' or 'barbaric' people from other parts of the world fuelled the sense of European superiority.

15

Government of race: Nazi Germany

After World War One, an atmosphere of social and economic depression existed in Europe. In this unstable climate, **fascist** (extremist) political ideas flourished. **Anti-Semitic** thinking became widespread across Europe and America. Anti-Semitism also surfaced in South Africa, underlying the ideas of racial **segregation** that separated black and white **communities**. In Germany, the writings and rousing speeches of a young politician called Adolf Hitler began to attract attention.

In a book called *Mein Kampf* (My Struggle), Hitler blamed Germany's economic problems on 'cretins, criminals, Jews, Gypsies, mixed-race Negroes and the feeble-minded'. Using ideas of **Social Darwinism**, Hitler falsely claimed that the **Aryan** (racially 'pure') culture of Germany was 'stronger' and must 'dominate'. He said that the non-Aryan races, particularly Jewish people, were trying to weaken and destroy the 'Volk' (Germanic race).

Racist laws

When the Nazi Party came to power in Germany in 1933, Hitler's 'vision' was spread through **propaganda** – speeches on the radio, articles in newspapers and even children's nursery rhymes. But it was laws made by the Nazis that confirmed Germany's government of race. These included the Nuremberg Laws on Citizenship and Race (1935), which banned 'inter-racial' marriage, forced non-Aryans to use separate seats, for example, on buses and park benches, and ruled that non-Aryans could not vote. The Nuremberg laws also deprived German Jews of their right to German citizenship.

Government officials in Nazi Germany measured facial features to find out whether or not people were of 'Aryan' descent.

Kristallnacht

One night in November 1938, mobs of angry protestors took to the streets to avenge the death of a German diplomat, alleged to have been murdered by a young Jewish man in Paris. In all, 91 people were killed, while synagogues, shops and homes were destroyed. So much shattered glass covered the streets the following morning that the night became known as Kristallnacht ('Night of Broken Glass').

In the months that followed Kristallnacht, all Jews were forced to wear a yellow 'Star of David' sewn on to their clothes. In the face of such harassment and **discrimination**, many fled to seek refuge in Britain, the USA and France. Many of those who remained were forced into **ghettos** and **concentration camps**. In 1942, at the Wannsee Conference, the Nazis made final plans to exterminate all Jewish people in Europe. This 'Final Solution' led to Jews being sent to execution camps in Poland and Germany. Only after the end of World War Two did people find out that more than six million Jewish children, men and women had been killed.

Not only did the Nazis divide society, they also systematically organized the mass killing of Jewish people. Forced to wear the Star of David, these families arrive at Auschwitz death camp in 1944.

'Separate Development' in South Africa

As the world recovered from the shock of **genocide** in Europe, the Afrikaner Nationalist Party (ANP) gained support for ideas of 'apartheid' (or 'apartness') in South Africa. The ANP won the 1948 election in South Africa with slogans suggesting that 'white civilization' mustn't disappear under a 'black sea'. In 1950, the Population Registration Act put all the people into racial categories. Inter-racial marriage was made illegal, and non-whites were not allowed to vote or join political parties. Soon the whole of South African society was involved in 'separate development', with separate housing, transport, drinking fountains, schools and healthcare for whites and non-whites. Though the black population made up more than 75 per cent of South Africa's total population, black people were only allowed to use 13 per cent of the land. The white population, which made up less than 15 per cent of the total population, was allocated 87 per cent of the land.

Resisting racism

While apartheid divided South African society, a growing **civil rights** movement responded to racism in the USA. How, asked African-American activists, could the USA promote a system of racial injustice, especially after having helped to defeat Hitler's government of race? How could the USA still enforce '**Jim Crow' laws** that had, for example, stopped black children attending state schools since the end of the American Civil War?

'We shall overcome'

These questions were not new. Since the beginning of the 20th century, political and **civil rights** groups had been working to combat racism in the USA. Since 1909 the National Association for the Advancement of Coloured People (NAACP) had held regular meetings and published their own magazine. But after World War Two, a wave of civil rights activity spread across the USA.

In 1947, the Congress of Racial Equality (CORE) organized the first 'Journeys of Reconciliation' (also known as 'Freedom Rides'). The idea was to challenge the **segregation** on public transport, particularly in southern states of the USA. CORE sent eight white men and eight black men to travel on public buses across Kentucky, Tennessee, North Carolina and Virginia. A number of the black activists were arrested several times for using whites-only transport. These journeys made the headlines in newspapers, on television and on radio throughout USA. This publicity encouraged other groups, such as the Southern Christian Leadership Conference (SCLC, founded in 1957) and the Student Nonviolent Coordinating Committee (SNCC, founded in 1960) to organize demonstrations and **boycotts** that challenged racial inequality. These included 'sit-in' protests at restaurants for whites only, more freedom rides on buses and trains, and 'freedom schools' that taught black history and challenged **discrimination** in American society.

Some of the greatest achievements were made in the law courts. For example, in the 1954 Brown versus Board of Education case, the Supreme Court decided that racial segregation in schools was against the Fourteenth Amendment of the US Constitution (the amendment promised protection by the government if a citizen's rights are threatened). This was a great boost for civil rights, and encouraged a school in Little Rock, Arkansas to become the first non-segregated central high school in 1957.

A beacon for the world

In 1963, 200,000 people marched in a peaceful demonstration to Washington, DC. They were protesting against segregation laws that still existed in parts of the USA. It was here that civil rights leader Martin Luther King Jr. gave his inspirational 'I Have a Dream' speech. In 1964, US Congress passed the Civil Rights Act, which made discrimination in public places illegal. This was an inspiration for many people in the USA: Hispanic **communities**, Native Americans and those who challenged other kinds of discrimination such as **sexism** and **homophobia**. By now, the rest of the world was listening too. In 1960s Australia, freedom rides similar to those that had taken place in the USA showed that Aboriginal people also experienced racism.

The Freedom Rides didn't go unchallenged by racist groups in the US. After being surrounded by a mob of white people near Anniston, Alabama in May 1961, this bus was firebombed.

❝I have a dream that my four children will one day live in a nation where they will not be judged by the colour of their skin but by the content of their character.❞

Martin Luther King Jr., (1963).

Martin Luther King Jr. at the centre of a civil rights march in 1960s America.

Our multi-ethnic world

People have been **migrating** all over the world for centuries. They may be fleeing natural disaster, racial **segregation** or war, or seeking out economic opportunity and an improved standard of life. Whether they migrated originally because of the Atlantic Slave Trade, or as Jewish people fleeing persecution, or as colonialists in Australasia and Africa, this movement of peoples explains why places like New York in the USA or London in the UK are so diverse.

A diverse society is made up of people with varying ethnic backgrounds. This diversity is often described as 'multi-ethnic', 'multiracial' or 'multicultural'. We can use these 'buzz-words' to describe the neighbourhood, town, city or the country we live in. Society benefits from this ethnic diversity in many ways: in music, in business, on the sports field and in politics. It makes all our lives richer and more interesting, extending our range of tastes, ideas, arts and beliefs.

When people describe themselves as British, Australian, Hispanic American, Australian Jewish or British-born African, they're often explaining who they are and where they come from. And it's just as important for a country to have an identity. Take, for example, Australia's identity as a land of opportunity for everyone. Many Australians may describe it as a 'fair go' or 'lucky' country. Or take the inscription on New York's Statue of Liberty that says: 'Give me your tired, your poor, Your huddled masses yearning to breathe free'. These ideas help us understand what kind of society we believe we live in, and whether it's fair and equal.

Actors Denzel Washington and Halle Berry triumph at the 2002 Academy Awards. Halle Berry was the first black woman to win Best Actress in the 74 year history of the Oscars.

Ethnic diversity

• Ethnic minorities, including people of non-British European descent, make up over 10% of Britain's population – more than 5 million people. Black people make up 6.2% of the population of England, 1.5% of the population of Wales and 1.3% of the population of Scotland. In London, black people make up one-fifth of the population.

• The diversity index was created in the USA to measure how racially and ethnically diverse the population is. In 2000, the diversity index was 49. That means that the chances of two randomly chosen US residents being from different ethnic backgrounds is 49 out of 100, or almost 1 in 2.

• Around 16% of Australians speak a language other than English at home. The most common are Italian, Greek, Cantonese, Arabic and Vietnamese. Australians speak more than 200 languages overall, including 48 Australian **indigenous** languages.

Tension in the melting pot

Across the world, many societies are now multi-ethnic. Some are more successful than others in achieving internal peace and equality, but everywhere there are problems encouraged by small groups of right-wing extremists. In Britain after World War Two, immigrants from the old British empire (referred to as the Commonwealth of Nations) came to the country in response to a demand for labour, only to meet with widespread **discrimination** when seeking jobs, housing and services. At first, politicians ignored the problem, despite violence against West Indians in the late 1950s in Nottingham and London. But then governments from 1962 onwards responded with a series of laws tightening control over immigration.

In 1968, a Labour government moved to deny entry to British citizens of Indian descent from East Africa, and a Conservative politician, Enoch Powell, made an intensely hostile and much publicized speech against the newcomers. The extreme right-wing British National Front (BNF) group supported him. There were similar outbursts in 1976. An anti-racist reaction produced **legislation**, the Race Relations Acts of 1968 and 1976, which outlawed discrimination and incitement to racial hatred. There has also been much local and voluntary effort to combat racism.

What about today?

Today there is still widespread discrimination in employment, and racial violence and harassment continue to be a problem. 'Hate crimes', such as physical attacks, verbal abuse or racially motivated murders, happen all over the world, though sometimes they go unreported. In the USA, the African-American statesman Colin Powell may be one of the most powerful leaders in the White House, but ordinary US citizens like Rodney King (see page 25) are still attacked and even murdered because of the colour of their skin.

Across Europe, political parties like the Front Nationale (FN) of France, the Austrian Freedom Party (FPO) or Danish Peoples' Party (DPP) blame immigration for social problems, sometimes adding that all African, Asian and Arab Muslim people should be 'sent home'. The Internet is used to send racist messages across the world, while in Europe racist groups use fire-bombs and nail-bombs to attack ethnic minorities. In Australia, some Aboriginal **communities** don't believe their country is 'fair go', because they don't have equal access to education, housing or healthcare. And after the attack, on 11 September 2001, on the World Trade Centre in New York, Muslim communities in the USA and Europe have experienced increased hostility.

There were 25,000 mourners at the funeral of a Turkish woman who was killed, along with four others, in a racist firebomb attack in the German town of Solingen. The peaceful funeral later became violent when some members of the crowd, unable to contain their anger and outrage, overturned cars, looted shops and smashed windows.

Crimes of hate

• In the year 2000, 9430 hate crimes were reported to law enforcement agencies in the USA.
• 65% of these crimes were directed at individuals, while 34.4% were against property.
• 32.1% occurred in or around residential properties, while 17.4% occurred on the street or on highways.
• Between 1995 and 1996, there were 12,199 racial attacks reported to the police in the UK.
• Between 1992 and 1996, eighteen people lost their lives in racial attacks in the UK.

Racism and the legal system

Most people experience the legal system in a variety of ways. It could be anything from an encounter with a neighbourhood police officer or judge in a courthouse, to the way in which prisons are run or governments handle drug problems. If racism affects any part of this legal system, peoples' **civil rights** are threatened and entire **communities** may lose faith in justice and feel excluded from society.

Racial profiling

The police use a system called profiling to deter criminals. This means that the police are allowed to stop and search any person they suspect of criminal activity. In Britain, a recent government study shows that black people are almost six times more likely to be stopped and searched than white people. This evidence of 'racial profiling' supports those communities who accuse the police of **discrimination**. And because it happens on the street – face-to-face – it can generate a lot of anger among ethnic minority communities.

In police custody

When a person is stopped or arrested by a member of the police force, it means that they are in 'police custody'. Occasionally people are injured, or even killed, while in police custody. The **human rights** group, Amnesty International, has claimed that, in Austria, police aren't likely to be taken

Caught on camera – when home video footage of Rodney King being beaten by a police officer was shown on TV, it sent shock waves across the USA.

to court if they assault members of ethnic minorities while they are in custody. Whereas, if a white person is assaulted, an officer is more likely to go to court. This inequality can create racial tension in society. For example, in the USA in 1991, four police officers were accused of assaulting Rodney King, a black US citizen, while he was in police custody. An amateur video of the attack was used as evidence against the police officers when the case was brought to court. Despite this evidence, which had also been broadcast throughout the USA on news programmes, the jury decided to **acquit** three of the officers. This decision sparked violent rioting in Los Angeles, which resulted in 2000 injuries, four deaths and US$990 million worth of damage.

When the system fails

Communities have often criticized the police for not taking racist crimes seriously enough. In the UK in 1992, a teenager called Stephen Lawrence died as the result of an unprovoked racist attack. The police were slow to find and convict the killers, so Lawrence's family decided to start their own investigation. Although the Lawrences didn't manage to convict the suspects, their efforts drew attention to the police handling of the case. The British government began to ask why the police had acted so unprofessionally. In 1999, a government inquiry accused the British police force of institutional racism.

❝This society has stood by and allowed my son's killers to make a mockery of the law.❞

Doreen Lawrence, mother of Stephen Lawrence, speaking about the UK government inquiry in 1999.

Stephen Lawrence's parents, Doreen and Neville, refused to accept the way in which the police had dealt with their son's death.

Racism at work

Race relations laws have made racial **discrimination** at work unlawful. Most companies also know that it is better for business to employ people that reflect the society as a whole. In a diverse society, companies do better if equal opportunities are given to people of all ethnic backgrounds. But despite this, the facts show that racial discrimination still exists at work.

For example, in Britain between 1999 and 2000, the number of college and university degrees rose among the black **community** more than it did among the white community. But in the same year, 12 per cent of the black population was unemployed, compared with 5 per cent of the white population. In the mid-1990s, there were more than 1300 registered cases of people who alleged they'd been racially discriminated against. Out of all these cases, 325 were settled out of court and 72 were decided in court, with an average compensation of £2750. Although racism at work can sometimes be difficult to notice, most of these cases are examples of direct discrimination.

Direct discrimination

An organization monitoring equal opportunities opened a telephone hotline to find out about racism at work. In just five days they had received 450 calls. A British black civil servant described how he'd been turned down for promotion, despite having the right qualifications. He discovered that a white person, with no qualifications, had got the job. When he complained, he eventually got the job, but his boss said how much he 'hated the black race coming in here to take jobs'. This upset the civil servant a great deal, especially since he'd been living in Britain for nearly 40 years. Another call was from a machine operator, who said people at the factory he worked at called him racist names. He had been forced to start working the night shift to avoid harassment.

These examples of direct racism are very stressful to those people who experience them. Some people become so depressed that they have to leave their jobs or take days off to recover. This is bad for the atmosphere of any workplace, and bad for business too.

"We want our kids in offices, not out with shovels."

A slogan used by a group of mothers speaking on behalf of their Aboriginal community who demanded better jobs for their sons and daughters. The mothers were attending a conference called the 'Indigenous Women's Forum' held in New South Wales, Australia in 2001.

Racism and sport

Sport can bring people together. It's a chance for raw ability to speak louder than racial **prejudice**. Sport is also a part of a country's 'cultural fabric', something that people talk about and share experiences of at school and work, on buses, trains and street corners. Some people would even say that sport is like a religion. Of course, sport is also about winning, but the greatest sports personalities – from Muhammad Ali to Tiger Woods – often talk about the atmosphere and the spirit of sport. And it's this spirit that can be spoiled by racism.

Tiger Woods, widely regarded as the best golfer of all time, is presented with the ceremonial green jacket after winning the US Masters tournament for the third time in 2002.

However, sometimes athletes themselves can display racist behaviour. In the build-up to the Sydney Olympics in 2000, an Australian athlete said: 'You can pretty much knock out all the dark guys'. He was referring to the fact that the conditions in Australia were better for him (a white athlete) than for black Americans. The Australian Olympic Committee apologized for the remark, but an American athlete said it would 'create animosity between the USA and Australia'. And there was the instance of an American Major League baseball player, who was not even talking about sport, but who offended people by saying: 'The biggest thing I don't like about New York are the foreigners. I'm not a very big fan of foreigners'.

In sports like American football, although ethnic diversity exists on the pitch, is it as diverse behind the dressing-room door? In 1999, for example, out of 31 head coaches in the US National Football League, only three were from ethnic minorities.

Most football fans follow the game for the love of it. But a very small minority see it as an opportunity to stir up racial hatred.

"There's no place for racism at school, football or anywhere in society. It's up to all of us to work together to stamp out racism."
Andy Cole, black Manchester United and England striker (2001).

The media and race

In a 'multimedia age', the images on television and cinema screens and the information we read in newspapers or on the Internet shape our opinions and our societies. Racism can be a part of the media in different ways. There are examples of direct racism on the Internet, shown through the growth of 'hate-sites'. Certain kinds of language used by news reporters can stir up an atmosphere of racial tension in society (see pages 32–3). And it is commonly the case that television and radio programmes don't reflect the diversity of society. Although people like Oprah Winfrey, Bill Cosby or Will Smith are very successful the media still tends to be dominated by white people. One reason for this is that the companies that pay to advertise their products in the media direct their adverts at wealthier sectors of society where there are smaller percentages of people from ethnic minorities.

These advertisers believe that white viewers are less likely to watch shows with majority black or hispanic casts.

Racial stereotypes

The people and characters we see on television or in the movies are often role models for us. But in the USA, for example, members of the Hispanic **community** complain that they are **stereotyped** by being given small or negative roles like criminals or drug dealers. Similar criticism has been directed at Australian television for stereotyping Aboriginal communities. And, even after the end of apartheid in South Africa, an independent government organization called the Human Rights Commission recently criticized the media for regularly using racial stereotypes and not taking news stories about some communities very seriously.

The cast of Friends. Many people feel that popular TV shows should reflect diversity in society, but this doesn't always happen.

Trouble at the top?

Who decides what sort of programmes should be on television, or what kind of characters will be in the movies? These decisions are made by 'people at the top' – producers, scriptwriters, news reporters and directors. The results don't mean that these people are racist, but simply that they don't reflect the diversity of society.

For example, in 2001, Greg Dyke of the BBC said that the organization was 'hideously white'. There are far more white people than black or Asian people working at the BBC, and this means that characters on television can become stereotyped, and the programmes may be out of step with the diverse nature of society. Dyke's criticism suggested that most high-ranking executives and producers are too often white (and male).

Oprah Winfrey has become one of the most powerful and wealthy media figures in the USA.

‚‚...every form of media is failing to deliver an accurate picture of our diverse society, and because of this, some of our citizens are slow to understand and accept other cultures.‚‚

Sir Herman Ouseley, Chairman of the UK Commission for Racial Equality.

The media and migration

There are many reasons why people move away from their homes. Some have fled war or racial persecution in their own countries, others are escaping poverty or want to improve life for themselves and their families. The reasons differ from person to person, but the arrival of **migrants** into countries is a hotly debated issue. Politicians might ask: 'Will immigrants put a strain on society?' 'Or do they improve an economy and enrich culture?' The media also fuel the debate, with images of people crossing the border from Mexico into the USA, or reports about refugees arriving in boats off the Australian coast. The 'heat' of these debates can create tension in society, and sometimes media coverage doesn't help.

A hostile reception

In 1998, **Roma** and **Kosovan** migrants began to arrive in the UK from Eastern Europe. Many were fleeing persecution in their own countries and seeking political asylum. In October 1998 a local newspaper in the south of England began publishing articles that said: 'We are left with the backdraft of human sewage and no cash to wash it down the drain'. The articles called the migrants 'bootleggers, scum-of-the-earth drug smugglers', and the newspaper defended its stance, saying it was 'their right to freedom of speech', and 'reflecting the opinion of the area'. Soon, national newspapers began to print similar articles. Some accused the government of 'going soft', and not doing enough to 'stem the tide' of migrants and asylum-seekers.

Border officials try to control the flow of people crossing between Mexico and the USA.

Can words create violence?

At the same time, there was an increase in the number of attacks on migrant families. Some had fireworks put through their letterboxes or bottles smashed against their windows. One house even had 'We will burn you' painted on it. This sort of violence began to happen in other parts of the UK. Often the victims weren't even migrants, they'd been attacked because of how they looked. Then, in August 2000, an asylum-seeker was murdered and two others were stabbed, all within three days of one another.

In April 2001, a **European Union** report was published that criticized the British media for the way in which they reported the arrival of migrants. It said that an atmosphere of racial tension had been created by 'intolerant coverage of these groups of persons in the media'. In 2002, Kris Janowski, the **United Nations** High Commissioner for Refugees told the French news agency, Agence France Presse, that: 'We do think there is a linkage between the notoriously negative portrayal of asylum-seekers in the media and this kind of violence.'

Young Muslims gather in Australia in August 2001. They are asking the Australian government to allow a ferry carrying 460 asylum-seekers from Afghanistan to land on Christmas Island.

Citizens of the world?

As societies around the world continue to become increasingly multi-ethnic, the arguments about racism become less about whether it is wrong or right. Instead the most pressing problem is how to ensure that diverse **communities** live without racial tension, in a society free of racial **prejudice** and **discrimination**. This chapter looks at the different opinions and arguments that have surfaced in the search for a multi-ethnic society in which *everybody* has equal opportunities in life.

A Red Cross 'holding station' accommodates refugees in Sangatte, northern France.

Today there are 150 million people living outside their countries of birth. At least 22 million have been forced to move from their homes because of war or racial persecution. We already know that the multi-ethnic societies are built on a history of migration. We also know that the arrival of **migrants** into a society can create racial tension. Some people argue that this tension is the result of a new kind of racism: that of discrimination and prejudice against people who want and need to improve their lives. But whether migration actually does create tension depends on the actions of governments across the world.

Managing migration

Since most of the migrant populations are from less developed countries, some people argue that they bring unskilled and uneducated individuals into society. If migrants have less 'economic value', there might be more strain on public services like health, housing and education. In the USA, for example, economists argue that if the government supports healthcare for Hispanic migrants, then others in society will have to pay more for health insurance. There is also a concern that migrants will become 'second-class' citizens, and that **ghetto**-like communities will grow. This division could mean that certain communities are excluded and less likely to become involved in the rest of society. To avoid this, some people think that governments should manage migration by limiting the number of people allowed in to a country. They think that governments should only select those individuals who fit the needs of a society – for example, those with skills, like doctors or computer experts, who can immediately contribute to the economy.

However, some people argue that managed migration makes matters worse. If only skilled migrants are encouraged, then there will be fewer people in less developed countries where the skills are needed most. This could lead to more poverty and even more people wanting to leave. The **United Nations** also estimates that, by the year 2025, 159 million migrant workers will be needed to keep the European economy growing. This is because birth rates in Europe are falling and there is a need for both skilled and unskilled workers. To keep the European economy growing, and to offer improved lifestyles for those in less developed countries, some argue that it is more sensible to relax migration controls and allow people to move more freely as citizens of the world.

Institutional racism

The term 'institutional racism' was first used by the American activist Stokely Carmichael during the US **civil rights** movement in the 1950s and 1960s. Institutional racism means that racism can exist anywhere in an organization, from the daily running of a small business to the way in which people are treated in a large concern such as the criminal justice system. Institutional racism may be evident in the lunch canteen at work, where racist jokes or **stereotypes** are accepted by employees. It might also mean that the opportunities people have while working for an organization are unequal. Or it may mean that a police force is prejudiced in the way in which it investigates crime within a certain **community**.

Too much pressure?

Some politicians and journalists argue that if a police force is accused of institutional racism, then it's even less likely that ethnic minorities will want to work for it. They also say that instructing the police force to 'clean up its act' can put too much pressure on officers. For example, after the Stephen Lawrence case in Britain, a police chief admitted: 'We failed. We could and should have done better'. But, according to critics, the media attention and public pressure that followed the Lawrence enquiry actually led to an increase in the number of street crimes affecting all citizens. Another leading police official said that: 'Officers' jobs have been made far more difficult.... Police are there to deal with crime; they are not interested in race'.

A Moroccan worker is detained by Spanish police following an increase in racial tension and unrest in the town of El Ejido in February 2000.

The UK police force has attempted to recruit a variety of ethnic groups as a way of representing the diversity of society and improving relations with citizens.

In the USA there are similar arguments in support of racial profiling. Those people in favour of profiling ask: if more crime is being committed by a certain **ethnic group**, then why is it wrong for a police force to use its limited amount of money and time to stop and search people of a particular ethnic group? If, for example, most drug dealers in an area are known to be black or Hispanic, then more ethnic minorities will show up in the crime figures. These arguments often say that racial profiling is justified, especially if the 'greater good' of society is at stake. But critics of racial profiling say it is an example of institutional racism because it is an everyday police practice that also targets innocent people because of the colour of their skin.

Although there is disagreement about the ways in which institutional racism should be handled, many people still believe that its 'discovery' is a positive step towards tackling **discrimination**. This is mainly because it has brought attention to racist crime in society and challenged discrimination inside large organizations like the police force and the criminal justice system.

"The collective failure of an organization to provide an appropriate and professional service to people because of their colour, culture, or ethnic origin. It can be seen or detected in the processes, attitudes and behaviour which amount to discrimination through unwitting prejudice, ignorance, thoughtlessness and racist stereotyping which disadvantage minority ethnic people."

Following the death of Stephen Lawrence, a government investigation resulted in a report (quoted above) that accused the UK police force of institutional racism.

Too black and white?

Some people still think our understanding of racism is too simplistic, often because there is evidence of racism *between* ethnic minorities. For example, there are cases of racial tension between African migrants and British-Caribbean communities in London, or examples of African-American schoolchildren calling Chinese-American students names. These examples show that racism is not just a 'black and white' issue, and that it's also important to look for other causes of racial tension that are rooted deep in society.

Society in the spotlight

Some people argue that not everyone in society is given an equal chance to go to school, find a good job or live in a comfortable home. This doesn't just mean inequality for ethnic minorities, it means inequality for poorer white **communities** too. If people can't find work or send their children to a good school, then a whole community might become depressed. This atmosphere of social depression can lead to more crime and unemployment. When something like this happens to a community, it is less likely that different **ethnic groups** will **integrate** because they blame each other for their problems.

People waiting in line for a 'soup kitchen' to open in 1991. Scenes of social depression like these have a negative impact on any community, and can also break down relations between different ethnic groups.

When society is **segregated** like this, relations between the different communities can break down even more quickly and easily, since they have less chance of learning to understand and accept each other. These sorts of problems are often deeply rooted in society, and can take a long time to change. Some people, however, believe that very practical and immediate things can be done. If a community is ethnically diverse, then there should be politicians, police, teachers, doctors and lawyers who reflect this diversity. If, for example, there were more British-Caribbean police or Hispanic police officers in certain areas of the UK or USA, then a lot of problems and tensions could be resolved before they became another ugly crime figure. This could help restore trust, forging stronger relations between all ethnic groups and helping to build a society where all people are treated fairly, with equal chances to achieve and feel proud about their lives.

Positive action – a black female police officer distributes anti-drugs literature to children.

❝...racism resides not so much in institutions, but in the hearts and minds of individuals.❞

Journalist Ziauddin Sardar talking about schools in East London, from a New Statesman magazine article (1999).

The global community against racism

Since the end of World War Two, the **United Nations** has been actively involved in the promotion of **human rights**. In 1948 the UN produced a Universal Declaration of Human Rights (part of it is quoted on page 4) which set new standards. It was followed by a series of more detailed agreements, such as the International Convention on the Elimination of All Forms of Racial Discrimination (1966). The UN has a committee that receives reports from governments and voluntary bodies on the progress being made under this Convention in different states. But the UN does not have any powers of enforcement.

There are also hundreds of non-governmental organizations (NGOs), such as Amnesty International and Human Rights Watch, which are dedicated to tackling racism. These organizations are independent of governments and carry out their own research into racism. Although they don't have the power to make laws, NGOs have a big influence in providing information to governments, and to the population as a whole. They work closely with the media, providing information and encouraging newspaper articles and television programmes that discuss racism. NGOs also offer support and legal advice to **communities** and individuals affected by racism. The presence of NGOs in society helps make people around the world more aware, and pressurizes governments to tackle racism.

❝...it can shape and embody the spirit of the new century, based on the shared conviction that we are all members of one human family.❞

United Nations High Commissioner for Human Rights, Secretary-General Mary Robinson, speaking at the World Conference Against Racism in South Africa in 2001.

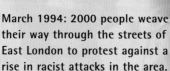

March 1994: 2000 people weave their way through the streets of East London to protest against a rise in racist attacks in the area.

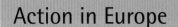

Action in Europe

The **European Union** has tried to promote anti-racist laws in all its member states for more than ten years. The law regarding racism in European countries varies greatly – currently the UK and the Netherlands have the most comprehensive and long-standing provisions. In May 2000, the Treaty of Amsterdam was agreed and came into force, after intense pressure from the **European Parliament** and NGOs. It stated that there could be European **legislation**, binding on all member states, against racial **discrimination**. This legislation is already in the pipeline. Racism in Europe is also monitored by an organization called the European Commission Against Intolerance and Racism (ECAIR), whose job is to promote awareness and offer advice to governments and people in Europe. It also carries out research into racism issues in each country. At the moment it is particularly active in tackling racism on the Internet, and has created an anti-racist website at www.ecri.coe.int.

The end of apartheid

The history of South Africa over the past hundred years is an example of how government based on racist beliefs can be defeated. From the moment that apartheid laws were introduced to **segregate** South African society in 1948, they were criticized by people from all walks of life in South Africa and across the world. In 1952, the **United Nations** formally condemned apartheid in South Africa. Throughout the 1950s and 1960s a growing number of protest marches were held in South Africa. Most were organized by the African National Congress (ANC), a group formed by black South Africans in 1912. The apartheid government opposed these demonstrations by banning the ANC, and putting leaders like Nelson Mandela in prison. But the struggle continued.

Sanctions

By the 1980s, the world's media was watching South Africa closely, and governments in Europe and the USA were beginning to put economic pressure (sanctions) on the country. Supported by the United Nations, these economic sanctions meant that most countries around the world stopped trading with South Africa. The racial violence worsened, and pressure from the international community increased. Eventually, in 1991, the South African president, F.W. de Klerk, lifted the ban on the ANC. At the same time, he began abolishing segregation laws and freed Nelson Mandela from prison (where he'd been for more than 25 years). Although the atmosphere in South Africa was still very tense, Mandela was now free to share his vision of a multi-racial, multi-ethnic future with the South African people and with the rest of the world. He called the new South Africa a 'Rainbow Nation'. In 1994, Mandela was elected president in the first multi-racial, democratic elections in South Africa. Although he left office in 1999, he continues to be one of the most inspiring leaders in the world today.

Truth and reconciliation

In 1996, the multi-ethnic South African government made a new constitution that officially ended apartheid. Since then, one of the most important things that the government has done to help challenge racism is to set up the Truth and Reconciliation Commission (TRC). The TRC was founded in 1995 to help heal South African people of the apartheid years. It became an opportunity for people to find out what **human rights** abuses took place between 1950 and 1994. More importantly, it supports apartheid victims with financial aid and helps 'restore their dignity'. More recently the TRC has supported museums that show the history of apartheid. The hope is that South Africa's troubled past will not be forgotten by future generations.

Nelson Mandela, who was elected first black president of South Africa in 1994.

❝We have seen a miracle unfold before our very eyes.... Freedom and justice must become realities for all our people and we have the privilege of helping to heal the hurts of the past.❞

From the opening speech of the TRC, made by Archbishop Desmond Tutu in 1995.

Mrs Nohle Mohapi becomes the first witness to be sworn in at the Truth and Reconciliation Commission in South Africa in April 1996.

43

Who else is tackling racism?

Governments and members of the **United Nations** are not the only agencies helping to tackle racism. Politicians themselves recognize that the most effective opposition to racism is achieved by individuals or groups working within a **community**. Today there are literally millions of people around the world helping to challenge racism in their neighbourhood, on the Internet, in their schools, in their favourite sports and in the media.

In communities and schools

People don't just teach anti-racism in the classroom – there are examples throughout the world of how schools and youth clubs are tackling racism outside of lessons too. One example is of parents getting together to encourage more activities and anti-racist lessons. Another is of pupils from different schools organizing football matches or music concerts to raise money for charity and to promote anti-racism. This very thing happened in Scotland, after an area had experienced racial tension. An organization called 'Kick It Out' helped some local children to stage an anti-racism football tournament. And in Australia, pupils from New South Wales get together every year for a public speaking competition to celebrate their multi-ethnic schools. In the USA, the work of 'Artists Against Racism' has encouraged numerous talented musicians and actors to promote anti-racism messages and mount anti-racism concerts. In some US schools, an organization called ERASE challenges racism by organizing training and activities to promote equality in education.

On the Internet

There are plenty of websites dedicated to tackling racism. Sites such as www.worldracism.com, www.icare.to, or www.oneworld.net provide the latest news on racism issues and encourage anti-racist campaigns. There are also sites that encourage people to report racism to their local government. These are good places to find more information and advice on racism issues, with links to issues across the country. There are also schools and universities, from Pennsylvania in the USA and Newcastle upon Tyne in the UK, to Bangkok in Thailand and Melbourne in Australia, who provide information about racism and guides that help people deal with racism if they experience it first hand.

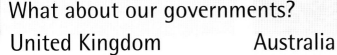

What about our governments?

United Kingdom

- In 2001, the Race Relations Act 2000 became law. This means that all organizations have a positive duty to monitor and promote racial equality. It also forbids public authorities to discriminate.
- During 2000, three important new measures to combat **discrimination** (based on Article 13 of the Treaty of Amsterdam) were adopted by the Council of Ministers of the European Union. For the first time, there will be a comprehensive set of anti-discrimination measures and a minimum standard of legal protection against discrimination throughout the European Union.

Australia

- In 1995, the Racial Hatred Act became law. This, combined with the 1975 Racial Discrimination Act, made it easier for people to complain about offensive or abusive behaviour.
- In 2002, a National Conference on Racism began to intensify anti-racist efforts in Australia over the next decade. It aimed to strengthen Australia's commitment to diversity.

The Music of Black Origin (MOBO) awards have become a major event in the UK music scene.

Ask yourself: Who am I?

By learning about the past and becoming more aware of racism issues today, everyone can become part of the **community** of people all over the globe who are challenging racism and intolerance. There are also many other, practical things that can be done to confront racism.

Racism reveals itself in facts and figures, but racist behaviour always begins with peoples' attitudes. And our attitude towards others is always rooted in who we are. One way to start thinking about who we are, is to trace our family tree. By asking ourselves who our grandparents or great-great grandparents are, we very quickly find that most peoples' backgrounds are not as straightforward as we might think. If, for example, a person decides to trace his or her ancestors at the local library or on the Internet, it can be difficult to answer questions such as: Am I black, white, mixed race? Am I British, Indian? Am I Australian, or American? By thinking about family history, people often find that they end up describing and understanding themselves in lots of different ways.

"As we are liberated from our own fear, our presence automatically liberates others."

Nelson Mandela in his inaugural speech as the first black president of South Africa in 1994.

Creating a tolerant community

There are many ways to bring anti-racism into a school or community. If, for example, there is racist graffiti on the walls in a neighbourhood, people often write letters to local politicians complaining and asking for it to be cleaned up. There are also lots of creative ways to tackle racism, like organizing a football tournament, play or music show to draw attention to the issue. Lots of people these days use the power of the Internet – they design anti-racist websites and offer information and useful contacts. And don't forget about the official, global anti-racism day on 21 March. Every year there are activities and events all over the world that are good fun, help people communicate how they feel about racism and create a deeper understanding of the issue.

Experiences of racism

If a person is physically attacked, or if his or her home, family or friends are attacked, he or she must report the incident to the police immediately. But, as this book has shown, racism is not always physical. If any sort of racial abuse is experienced, there are many people and organizations who can listen and help. The most important thing to remember is that racism is against the law in the UK, Australia, the USA, Europe, in fact, the world over. Though the laws vary slightly from country to country, it is everybody's right to challenge racism.

Who should I talk to?

Racism can be difficult to talk about. But, whether racism is experienced at school or in a **community**, there are always people close by who can help. One of the first things to do is write down the things that happen, noting the dates and places. This can help people express their fears, but this record may also be useful to help prove that racism has been experienced or witnessed. A teacher, a friend or someone in your family will always be there for you to listen and give advice. The same can be said if a friend or a neighbour is experiencing racism; being there to listen and talk helps people express their frustrations or fears.

What will happen when I speak to someone?

The action and advice people give depends on what sort of racism is experienced. Sometimes talking to a teacher, family or friend won't be enough, and in these cases a more official complaint may be necessary. This may sound daunting, but it's very important to report racial incidents so that they can be solved. If they're not reported, then racist behaviour can spread and could hurt someone else.

Who else can I contact?

There are lots of other people in the neighbourhood and organizations in this country that are dedicated to helping stop racism. If people find it difficult to talk to relatives or friends, then these organizations will provide support. It is worth looking in the local telephone book for organizations, or asking in a nearby library. There is also a list at the back of this book, suggesting people nearby who will gladly listen and help, and offering more advice and information.

Facts and figures

Hate crime and criminal justice

United Kingdom

• The British Crime Survey estimated that about 130,000 racially motivated crimes were committed against black and Asian people in 1997.

• In Britain, 18% of male prisoners and 24% of female prisoners are from ethnic minorities. One-third of all young black people in Britain come into contact with the justice system by their late twenties.

• Black and ethnic minority people are five times more likely than white people to be stopped and searched by the police. In London, 20% of the population are from ethnic minority groups, but they make up 43% of those stopped and searched.

Sources: Institute of BritKid; Race Relations; CARF; IRR

Australia

• The imprisonment rate for **indigenous** (Aboriginal or Torres Islander) adults in 1997 was more than fourteen times that for non-indigenous adults.

• In 1996, an indigenous youth was 21 times more likely to be detained in custody than a non-indigenous youth.

• In 1998, the rate of imprisonment for indigenous males aged 20–29 was 1 in 20, compared with 1 in 200 for non-indigenous males of the same age.

Source: Human Rights and Equality Commission, Australia

USA

• In 2000, 9430 hate crimes were reported to law enforcement agencies across the USA.

• 65% of these hate crimes were directed at individuals, while 34.4% were against property.

• 32.1% occurred in or around residential properties, while 17.4% happened on the street or on highways. Intimidation was the most frequently reported crime.

• In 1999, a report revealed that, out of 175,000 stop-and-search incidents over a fifteen-month period in New York, black people were six times more likely to be stopped by police.

• In 1999, a report in New Jersey revealed that out of all people stopped and searched by police, 77.2% were people of colour.

Sources: FBI; US Justice Dept; Human Rights Watch

Racism on the Internet

- In 1995, there was one racist website in North America, today there are more than 1400.
- The European Union reported 2100 hate-sites, with 300 based in Germany.
- Ethnic minorities and low-income families are the least likely people in society to own a computer and use the Internet.
- 13% of young black people and 12.1% of young Latino people in America have access to the Internet, compared with 35.8% of white youth.

Source: ECAIR; about.com

The rise of extremist politics in Europe

In September 2001, the **United Nations** Commission on Human Rights expressed a concern about the rise of extreme political groups: 'Neo-fascism and neo-Nazism are gaining ground in many countries – especially Europe.'

France – the right-wing Front Nationale won 17.9% of the vote during the second round of the French presidential elections in 2002.

Norway – the Progress Party, an anti-immigration party, won 14.6% of the 2001 general election vote.

UK – the British National Party, a neo-Nazi party, scored 11.4% of the local election votes in 2002.

Italy – in 1995, the National Alliance, formerly the post-war fascist Italian Social Movement, changed its name and scored 12% of the votes in the 2001 general election.

Austria – in 1999, the Freedom Party, an anti-immigration, anti-refugee party, scored 26.9% of the votes in the general election.

Source: OneWorld.org; IRR

Further information

Contacts in the UK

Amnesty International
99-119 Rosebery Avenue,
London EC1 4RE
Tel: 020 7814 6200
email:info@amnesty.org.uk
http://www.amnesty.org.uk

The Campaign Against Racism and Fascism (CARF)
BM Box 8784,
London WC1N 3XX
Tel: 020 7837 1450
email: info@carf.demon.co.uk
http://www.carf.demon.co.uk

ChildLine
Freepost 1111,
London N1 OBR
Tel: 0800 1111 (freephone)
email: reception@childline.org.uk
http://www.childline.org.uk

The Commission for Racial Equality (CRE)
Elliot House,
10-12 Allington Street,
London SW1E 5EH
Tel: 020 7828 7022
email: info@cre.gov.uk
http://www.cre.gov.uk

The Home Office
7th floor
50 Queen Anne's Gate,
London SW1H 9AT
Tel: 0870 0001585
email: public.enquiries@homeoffice.gsi.gov.uk
http://www.homeoffice.gov.uk

The Institute of Race Relations
2-6 Leeke Street,
King's Cross Road,
London WC1
Tel: 020 7833 2010 / 020 7837 0041
email: info@irr.org.uk
http://www.irr.org.uk

Kick It Out
PO Box 29544,
London EC2A 4WR
Tel: 020 7684 4884
email: info@kickitout.org
http://www.kickitout.org

NSPCC (National Society for the Prevention of Cruelty to Children)
National Centre,
42 Curtain Road,
London EC2A 3NH
Tel: 0808 800 5000 (freephone)
email:info@nspcc.org.uk
http://www.nspcc.org.uk

Contacts in the USA

American Civil Liberties Union
125 Broad Street, 18th Floor
New York, NY 10004
email: aclu@aclu.org
http://www.aclu.org/

Amnesty International USA
National Office,
322 Eighth Avenue,
New York, NY 10001
Tel: (212) 807-8400
http://www.amnesty-usa.org/

CORE (Congress of Racial Equality)
817 Broadway, 3rd Floor,
New York, NY 10003
Tel: (212) 598-4000
email: core@core-online.org
http://www.core-online.org/

US Department of Justice
950 Pennsylvania Avenue NW
Washington, DC 20530
Tel: (202) 514 3831
http://www.usdoj.gov

US Department of State
2201 C Street NW,
Washington, DC 20520
Tel: (202) 647 4000
email: Secretary@state.gov
http://www.state.gov/

Contacts in Australia

**Aboriginal and Torres Strait
Islander Commission**
PO Box 17,
Woden,
ACT 2606
Tel: (02) 6121 4000
http://www.atsic.gov.au/

Amnesty International
Private Bag 23,
Broadway,
NSW 2007
Tel: (02) 92 17 76 00
email: adminaia@amnesty.org.au
http://www.amnesty.org.au

Australian Lawyers for Human Rights
PO Box A147,
Sydney South,
NSW 1235
Tel: +61 2 9399 6153
email: alhr@alhr.asn.au
http://www.alhr.asn.au

**The Department of Immigration, Multicultural
and Indigenous Affairs (DIMIA)**
PO Box 25,
Belconnen,
ACT 2616
Tel: (02) 6264 1111
http://www.immi.gov.au

**The Human Rights and Equal Opportunities
Commission (HREOC)**
GPO Box 5218,
Sydney, NSW 1042
Tel: (02) 9284 9600
Complaints infoline: 1300 656 419
Privacy hotline: 1300 363 992
General enquiries: 1300 369 711
email: complaintsinfo@hreoc.gov.au
http://www.hreoc.gov.au/

The Internet

The following websites deal with racism and
human rights issues today.

www.worldracism.com
www.racialharassment.org.uk
www.hrw.org
www.raceactionnet.co.uk
www.magenta.nl/crosspoint
www.coe.int/ecri
www.oneworld.net
www.racismnoway.com.au
www.igc.org
www.icare.to
www.britkid.org
www.lawstuff.org.au
www.un.org/cyberschoolbus/index.html

Further reading

Issues: Racism, Craig Donnellan (Editor)
(Independence, 1999)

*When Hate Comes to Town: Community
Responses to Racism and Fascism* (Searchlight
Educational Trust, 1995)

*Spreading Poison: A Book About Racism and
Prejudice*, John Langone (Little Brown & Co,
1993)

Global Issues: Racism, Samid Garg and Jan
Hardy (Hodder Wayland, 1996)

Why Pick On Me?, Maud Blair (Trentham Books,
2001)

Stand Up For Your Rights, Paul Atgwa (Two-Can
Publishing, 2001)

*Separate But Not Equal: The Dream and the
Struggle*, James Haskins (Scholastic, 2002)

Glossary

abolitionist
individual or group of people that actively campaigns for the end of an injustice, for example, slavery

acquit
free or release from a charge or a crime

anti-Semitic
term describing prejudice or hostility directed towards Jewish people

Aryan
originally refers to peoples speaking a mixture of European and Indian languages. The Nazi Party, however, falsely believed that the term referred to peoples of Scandinavian descent. They twisted this idea further to describe Aryans as the 'master race', which excluded Jews, Slavs and Africans. The theory was based on a false racial theory of the 19th century.

boycott
form of protest involving the breaking of links (for example, with a country) or not using a business or service

civil rights
legal and moral rights of people in a country

community
group of people who share the same interests in life

concentration camp
prison camp in which non-military prisoners (civilians) are held

democracy
political system in which a country's leaders are elected by the people

discrimination
unfair treatment of a person on the grounds that he or she belongs to a different ethnic group

DNA (deoxyribonucleic acid)
chemicals that carry qualities, potentials and physical characteristics from one generation to the next

dysentery
infection of the intestine

ethnic group
group of people who share the same national or cultural history

European Parliament
part of the decision-making apparatus of the European Union, made up of representatives elected by each of the member states

European Union
alliance between fifteen European countries, known as 'member states'

evolution
process that describes how living animals or plants change over time

fascist
person who believes in an extreme set of nationalist and militarist political views

genes
sequences in a biological cell that contain DNA

genetics
branch of biology that studies heredity and variation in life

genocide
deliberate and systematic destruction of an entire political or ethnic group

ghetto
originally a part of a city set aside for Jews; used loosely to mean a poor area with a majority of ethnic minority residents

homophobia
prejudice towards homosexual people

human rights
each person's right to liberty and justice

indigenous
originating from a country or region

Industrial Revolution
period during the 18th and 19th centuries when first Britain and then other European countries and the USA were transformed from farming into industrial nations

integrate
blend in with or co-operate with other ethnic groups in a society

Jim Crow laws
laws introduced at the end of the American Civil War that discriminated against African-American people. Such laws prevented black people from attending school and from using restaurants, theatres and public baths.

Kosovan
person or group of people from the Kosovo area within the republic of Serbia in former Yugoslavia.

legislation
process of making laws

migrant
person who moves from a town, city or county to settle in another

migrate
move from one area or country to another

minority
ethnic or other group that doesn't represent the majority in a neighbourhood, town, city or country

nationality
linking of a person's identity with a particular country

prejudice
fixed ideas about a person or group of people that aren't based on knowledge or fact

propaganda
use of the media to influence people's opinions

pseudo
false or fake

race relations
relationship between people that are said to be of different races or ethnic groups

Roma
person or ethnic group, originally from southern Asia. The term has recently come to be associated with people from Eastern Europe.

segregate
separation of different ethnic groups in society, especially in housing, education or transport

sexism
prejudice towards the opposite sex

smallpox
very contagious disease. The sufferer develops a high fever, and a rash of blisters, which eventually dry up to leave scars.

Social Darwinism
pseudo scientific theory based on the idea that ethnic groups and races are subject to the same laws of natural selection that Charles Darwin discovered in plant and animal life

species
individual animals or plants that have common biological attributes

stereotype
definition of a person according to his or her physical characteristics, regardless of that person's individual personality or abilities

United Nations
voluntary association of countries which join together to promote international peace and security

Index

Aboriginal people 12, 19, 23, 27, 30
Africa 10, 11, 12, 13, 17, 20
anti-Semitism 16, 54
apartheid 5, 17, 18, 30, 42–43
asylum-seekers 32, 33
Australia 23, 44, 45
  Aboriginal racism 19
  European rule 12, 13
  immigration 23, 32, 33
  indigenous people 27
  Italians 4
  laws 6, 48
  media 30
  sport 29
  white people 8

Britain 24, 26
  colonies 12
  ethnic minorities 21
  immigration 22, 33
  Jews 17
  slave trade 11, 55

Christianity 13
civil rights 6, 18, 19, 24, 36, 54
colonies 12, 13, 14, 20
concentration camps 7, 17, 54

Darwin, Charles 14, 15, 55
DNA 8, 9, 54

East Africa 10, 12, 13, 22
equal opportunities 26, 34
ethnic cleansing 5

Europe 41, 55
  apartheid 42
  anti-Semitism 16
  explorers 13
  immigration 23, 32
  Industrial Revolution 55
  Jews 17
  laws 6, 48
  migrants 35
  National Front 23
  slave trade 10

genetics 15, 54
genocide 5, 17, 54
Germany 5, 12, 16, 17
graffiti 4, 5, 47

heredity 8, 54
Hitler, Adolf 16, 18
human rights 4, 6, 40, 55
  abuses 43
  laws 24
  media 30

immigration 22, 32
indigenous people 27, 55
institutional racism 5, 25, 36-37

Jews 16, 17, 20, 54

King Jr., Martin Luther 19
King, Rodney 23, 24, 25
Kosovans 4, 32, 55

Lawrence, Stephen 25, 36, 37

Mandela, Nelson 7, 42, 43

missionaries 12, 13
Muslims 23, 33

National Front 22, 23
Native Americans 13, 19
Nazi Party 5, 16, 54

refugees 32, 33, 34
Roma people 4, 32, 55

slavery 10–11, 14, 54
South Africa 7, 40
  apartheid 5, 16, 17, 18, 30, 42, 43
stereotypes 4, 9, 30, 31, 36, 37, 55

UK 5, 23, 45
  diversity 20, 39
  European Union 41
  immigration 32, 33
  Kosovans 4
  laws 48
  police 37
USA 4, 9, 23, 44, 55
  apartheid 42
  civil rights 18, 19
  Civil War 11
  discrimination 23
  diversity 20, 39
  ethnic groups 21, 37
  immigration 32
  Jews 17
  laws 6, 48
  media 30
  migrants 35
  Native Americans 13
  Rodney King 24, 25